# TANGLE ART & DRAWING GAMES FOR KIDS

## JEANETTE NYBERG

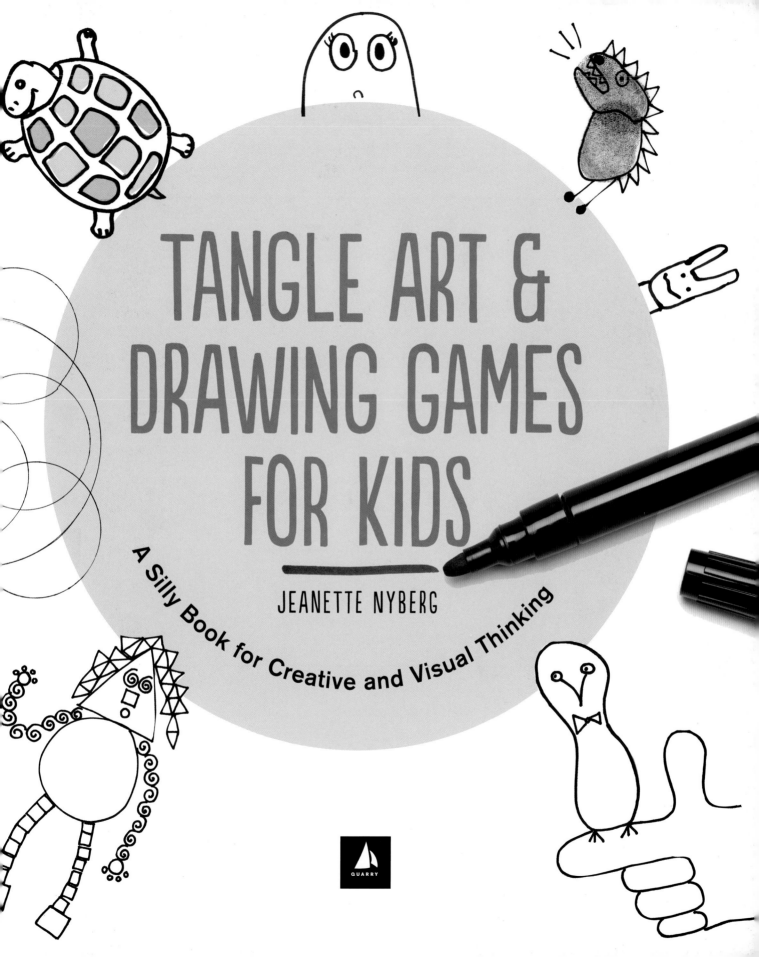

# TANGLE ART & DRAWING GAMES FOR KIDS

## JEANETTE NYBERG

A Silly Book for Creative and Visual Thinking

QUARRY

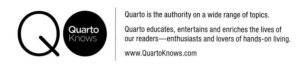

© 2016 Quarto Publishing Group USA Inc.
Text and illustrations © 2016 Jeanette Nyberg

First published in the United States of America in 2016 by
Quarry Books, an imprint of
Quarto Publishing Group USA Inc.
100 Cummings Center
Suite 406-L
Beverly, Massachusetts 01915-6101
Telephone: (978) 282-9590
Fax: (978) 283-2742
QuartoKnows.com
Visit our blogs at QuartoKnows.com

10 9 8 7 6 5 4 3 2 1

ISBN: 978-1-63159-126-6

Digital edition published in 2016
eISBN: 978-1-63159-191-4
Library of Congress Cataloging-in-Publication Data is available

Printed in China

Cover and Book Design: Laura McFadden
Cover Art: Jeanette Nyberg
Cartoon Illustrations: Shutterstock.com
Illustrations pages 56 and 57: Mike Wanke

For Christian, whose creativity is inspiring.

# Contents

**8** **Introduction**

## SIMPLE DRAWING GAMES 10

## GAMES WITH FRIENDS 34

# MIXED-MEDIA GAMES 58

**Chapter 3**

# AWESOME TANGLE GAMES 84

**Chapter 4**

# Introduction

 # YOU ARE A CREATIVE KID. RIGHT?

Even if you don't think you are, you have creativity running through your whole being, and you are totally cool because of it. Do you already like to doodle and draw? Maybe your homework looks a little like a sketchbook. Maybe you fill pages of paper with drawings. Or maybe you're a little intimidated by drawing.

Whatever the case, we're going to get you doodling and drawing all over the place and loving it. You won't even realize you're making art until it's too late, and you look down at your page and see that you've been moving that marker across the paper like you just can't stop.

Sometimes, we're all at a loss for what to draw—even if you're a voracious art-maker and you want every bit of drawing inspiration you can get your hands on.

Welcome to this book! On these pages, I present to you forty-six fantastic, amazing, mind-boggling drawing games and tangle exercises—enough to fill your days with creating forevermore.

Many of you have already found the powerful ways that focusing on drawing can calm you, center you, and open your mind. I think most of us who have ever found ourselves using a pen to draw cool patterns across a page can attest to the magical benefits of doodling.

In fact, one of the best things about drawing is that you needn't feel like you are artistically talented to take it up. It's open to everyone, and you merely need a pen and piece of paper to get started.

Most of the projects in this book have been created in such a way that you can do them even if you have zero confidence in drawing. Flip through and try one out! Start with the very easiest (and sometimes hilarious) drawing games in the beginning or jump into the games that use more than one medium—color is fun to explore. Finally, if you are looking for a more meditative way to spend your drawing time, throw on some music and tangle the day away with the projects in the third section.

*P.S. Always remember: All kids are creative; don't let that get away from you.*

*P.P.S. I bet your parents will want to do some of these with you.*

Here are some of the materials used in this book, and feel free to substitute if you like using a particular material or if you just don't have it handy.

- Permanent markers in fine and ultra fine points
- Colored markers—I use anything from Sharpies to Prismacolors, depending on the color and marker tip I like.
- Watercolor and brushes
- Ruler or straight edge
- Black drawing pens like Microns or Faber Castells
- Pencil

- Black india ink
- Blue painter's tape
- Ink pad
- Crayons or oil pastels

Chapter

1

# SIMPLE DRAWING GAMES

Most of these games require a pen or pencil. A ridiculous disposition will also help. (I know there's some silliness lurking inside of you!) As I was developing these projects, I couldn't stop thinking up new riffs on these ideas. Let yourself do the same and feel free to add your own crazy twists as you try these activities.

Flip through the book and try whichever games appeal to you at first glance. Some of them require (or can alternatively be done) with a partner, so enlist the help of your friends or family.

Whenever you find a drawing game that you particularly love, be sure to play it more than once. You will see how the games have different outcomes every time you try them. Grab a big stack of paper (I adore white card stock) and keep the fun flowing. There are usually an infinite number of ways to approach these games, and your third or fourth try might end up being your favorite!

# GEOMETRY TREE

This is a fun drawing exercise to try for an hour or so when your younger (or older) sister (or brother) is totally annoying you and you need to go slam your bedroom door and CHILL. Grab a fine point Sharpie.

"This beats hanging out with my sister any day."

**1** Starting near the bottom of the page in the middle, draw a vertical line that extends up about a quarter of the page. This line will be your "trunk."

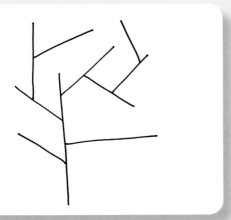

**2** Draw several straight lines or "branches" out from this trunk, taking your time and filling up the page.

**3** Begin to close up the open shapes with straight lines. Stop when you feel the need to stop. Wasn't that satisfying?

## More Fun

Close up the open areas with rounded lines, color in your shapes, doodle inside them, etc. This tree is a great starting point for lots more drawing!

# FISH LOOPS

Fish are fun to draw, especially when you cheat a little and make up your own fish. Who knows what's lurking at the bottom of the ocean?

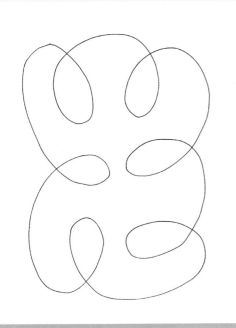

**1** Using a thin marker or pen, draw a big, loopy closed shape around the perimeter of your page.

**2** Turn all of the loops into fish. Blub, blub, blub.

# Make It Silly

Is your fish sticking out its tongue? Maybe it's wearing a mustache . . . or sunglasses, or socks. What?!?

"Blub"

"Blub"

"Blub"

# HORIZON DRAWINGS

Use this simple game to turn a weird jagged line into something awesome.

**1** Using a marker (I used a fine tip Sharpie), draw a jagged line horizontally across the middle of the page. As you draw, incorporate some shapes above the line and some below it.

**2** Now guess what you do! Turn the upper shapes into monsters!

"Despite my hair covering one eye, I can still see how awesome this looks."

## More Fun

Try this game again, only this time turn your line into different things—a cityscape, a strange caterpillar, etc.

# CUBE CONNECTIONS

Have you learned how to draw cubes? Sometimes it's hard to stop drawing them once you start, and then you wonder what could be more fun than drawing cubes. Connecting them with lines! Seriously. It's fun and relaxing and looks like a cool abstract mathematical work of art.

18

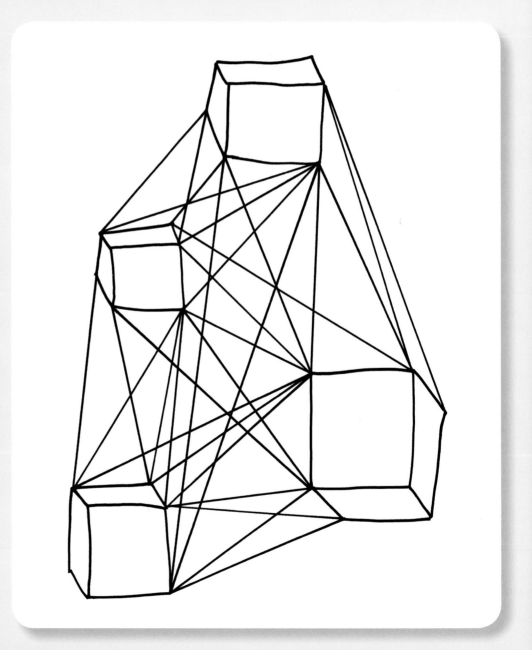

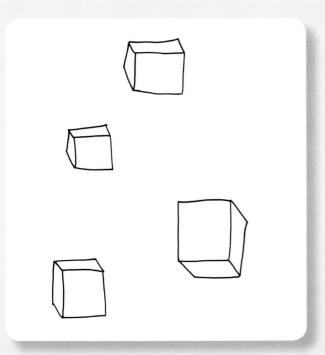

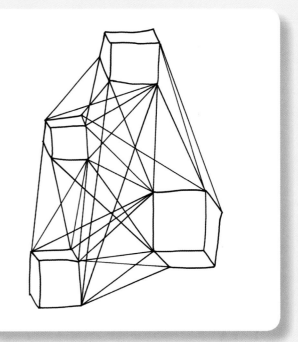

**1** Begin by drawing some cubes on the page, as many as you want, scattering them every which way across the page.

**2** Using your ruler, connect the cubes at the corners with straight lines. You decide how many lines you want and where to connect them. Don't think too hard about it; just start drawing and stop when you want to stop.

## More Fun

These boxes are just crying out to be colored in, aren't they. Or tangled. With this project, you can do it all!

"I am going to start a new art movement. I think I'll call it Cubism."

# EGG HEADS

It's fun to draw faces and even more fun to draw a whole group of faces together. Sit and draw a crowd and see how many expressions you can come up with.

**1** Across the bottom of your page, draw a row of oval tops. Continue up until you have your page covered with rows of oval tops as shown in this image.

**2** Fill in the expressions to make your very own family of egg heads.

# Make It Silly

I think you should probably cut out these egg heads, glue ice pop sticks onto the backs of them, and have a puppet show.

"Unfortunately, I will have to eat the whole box of the ice pops in order to do that."

# INITIAL DESIGNS

Your initials are personal, and they'll be with you through your entire life. Why not make them special by turning them into art?

**1** Practice writing your initials in print, cursive, all capitals, lowercase, and any other decorative style.

## More Fun

Design a business card for yourself using your favorite initials drawing as your logo.

**2** After you are warmed up a little, take it a step further, doodling around your initials, experimenting with bubble letters, and other embellishments.

# FIVE-DOT DRAWINGS

After trying this game once, don't be surprised if you find yourself doing this drawing game all the time. It's all about silliness.

**1** Draw five dots on the page, anywhere you want.

**2** Using a pencil (or pen if you're brave), draw a figure, using dot one as the head, dots two and three for the hands, and dots four and five as the feet.

"Maybe this same technique will work on my freckles."

# Make It Silly

Try drawing the figure with the feet where you think the hands should go and the hands where it looks like the feet should go. Now try to get into that pose. Ouch!

# HAND MONSTERS

You've probably traced your hand before, but have you ever made it into a monster?

**1** Trace around your four fingers, but not your thumb.

**2** Now use your finger tracing as a starting point to draw a monster.

# Make It Silly

This is pretty silly to begin with, but try turning your hand upside down and creating a fabulous sea creature monster.

"If I turn my whole body upside down, can I keep my hand right side up?"

SIMPLE DRAWING GAMES

# UPSIDE-DOWN DRAWINGS

For this game, you will hang upside down and draw.
Just kidding!

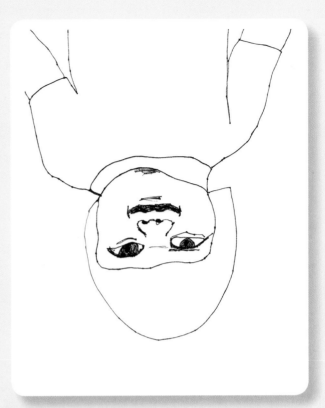

**1** Find a photograph of something or someone and turn it upside down on the table in front of you.

**2** Now draw that image on your page. You'll have to really look at what you're drawing—it feels a lot different than drawing things as you normally see them, doesn't it?

## Tip
While you are drawing, try to forget exactly what it is that you are drawing. Instead, think of it as a bunch of lines that you are trying to copy.

"Hey, how'd I do that? I am awesome."

# DRAW WITH YOUR FOOT

As if upside-down drawing weren't weird enough, now let's try drawing with our feet! You may want to plug your nose when you remove your sock.

**2** Laugh until your stomach hurts. (Can you tell that this drawing is my dog asleep in front of the couch? No? Okay.)

**1** Grasp your pen or pencil with your toes and draw something or someone.

"Now I can play video games while I draw with my feet."

## Make It Silly

Wouldn't it be even more silly to try to draw using both feet at the same time? Or to try drawing the same thing at the same time using one hand and one foot? You first!

# FIVE-CIRCLE MASTERPIECE

I must like the number five. This is similar to the Five-Dot Drawings game (page 24), but with a twist.

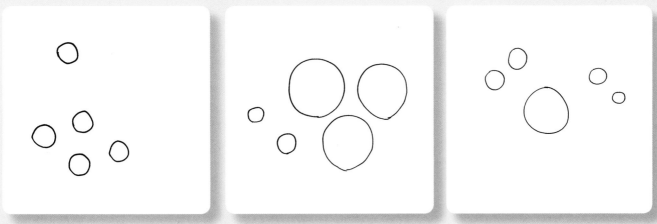

**1** Draw five circles on your page. Draw them anywhere and make them any size you like.

**2** Now, use those circles to make something. You can either make five different things or turn all five circles into one big thing—anything goes. (Sometimes it's fun just to draw five smiley faces.)

## More Fun

As you draw your circles, try to draw completely perfect circles. I bet you'll end up filling a page just trying to get one perfectly round.

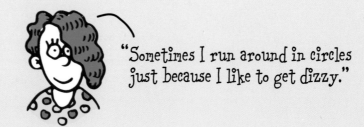

"Sometimes I run around in circles just because I like to get dizzy."

Chapter

2

# GAMES WITH FRIENDS

Question: How do you make drawing even more fun than you could ever imagine? Answer: Add a friend or three and tackle some of these games together! Snacks are optional, but highly recommended. I'll bet you can't get through one of these without lots and lots of laughing.

**Here are some other ideas:**

- If you are hanging out with a friend, take turns choosing games.

- After you try a game the basic way, always feel free to add your own creative twist. In fact, I CHALLENGE you to do this!

- If a friend isn't handy, parents are fine substitutes. (You will easily blow their minds with your skills and original thinking!)

# SYNCHRONIZED DRAWING

This project is designed for two people. You will need two pens or thin markers.

**1** Fold a line down the center of the page. Decide who will be the "leader" and who will be the "follower."

**2** Begin with your pens toward the top of the page, writing on either side of the line. The leader begins by drawing a shape out from the center and down toward the bottom of the page, without lifting the pen from the page. Do this fairly slowly because the follower is watching what is being drawn and trying to keep up while drawing the exact same thing! You can certainly try to draw a recognizable shape, but it's easier at first to stick with blobby blobs.

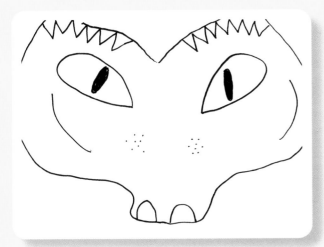

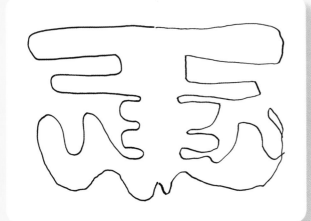

## Make It Silly

Remember how I said to draw slowly? If you speed up your drawing, the follower will find it harder to keep up, but it's really funny!

Game

# 13

# TOTEM CREATURES

Totem poles are the perfect object for this game. You can do this with as few as two people and as many as five.

**1** The first person starts at the bottom of the page, drawing one creature-face-type shape.

**2** Fold the page back and pass it to the next person, making sure you leave two marks where your creature left off.

**3** Continue until you get to the top of the page, where the last person finishes off the top of the totem creature.

## More Fun

Try doing this project on a giant piece of white paper from a roll.

"Follow my lead, little sister."

"Does that include following you and your friends around?"

# SHAPE INTERPRETATIONS

In this game, take turns interpreting the shapes your friend has drawn and have them do the same with your shapes.

40

**1** Using a pencil, draw some random closed shapes on a sheet of paper.

**2** Give it to your friend with an eraser and another pencil. Your friend can erase parts of the lines and use the pencil to turn your shapes into cool things.

## More Fun

Set rules about what each of you must draw, such as only draw foods! Make them all faces! Turn them into shoes!

"I'm turning these shapes into characters with attitude."

Game
15

# ROLL-THE-DICE SHAPE FIGURES

By limiting your drawing options to basic shapes, this game forces you to think beyond your go-to method for drawing body parts. Each player draws each of the ten body parts in the order listed below. The shape used to draw each part is determined by the roll of a die.

42

**1** To begin, players roll the die to determine which shape they will use to draw the first body part, which happens to be a head. Then players consult the chart to see what shape they should use. For example, if a three is rolled, that player will use a squiggly line to draw the head. Work your way through all ten body parts, rolling the die each time before beginning to draw.

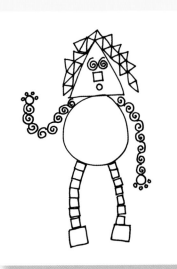  

**2** Each of you can draw separate people or collaborate on one person, taking turns with rolls of the die.

## Draw in this order:

1. Head                6. Arms
2. Nose                7. Legs
3. Eyes                8. Hands
4. Mouth               9. Feet
5. Torso               10. Hair

## Dice roll:

1. Square              4. Triangle
2. Circle              5. Straight Line
3. Squiggly line       6. Spiral

### Tip

You don't have to draw just one of any shape per body part. For example, if you roll a triangle, you can draw lots of them to make up the hair.

Game

16

# FRAME COLLABORATIONS

These are no ordinary frames!

44

"Did somebody say, 'Good looking?'"

1 You and a friend will draw a page of frames for each other.

2 Draw whatever sort of frame you like and add in one surprise element that your friend has to incorporate into his or her drawing.

## More Fun

Make the frames big—one per page—cut them out and decorate them, color them in, and hang them all over your house.

# FINISH A FIGURE WITH A FRIEND

Play this hilarious drawing game with a friend, taking turns drawing a face or figure.

**1** Fold your page in half, either horizontally or vertically.

**2** Draw one half of the face or figure—the left or right half if the paper is folded vertically or the top or bottom if it is folded horizontally. Continue drawing a quarter inch onto your partner's side of the page so they know where to begin. Have your friend finish the drawing on the other half of the page.

## More Fun

Try folding the page in different ways: quarters or thirds. Experiment!

# ROBOT STARTERS

There's never a bad time to draw robots, and really, never a bad way. Gather between two and five friends and see what crazy contraptions you come up with!

**1** Give each person a piece of paper and set a timer for 1 minute. Have players draw one part of a robot on their page.

**2** When the time is up, have players pass their pages to the person on their left (or just swap if there are two of you) and continue drawing for 1 minute.

**3** You can continue the game until the drawings seem complete. Even if there is a complete robot figure, you can continue to add exciting details and spare parts as you watch your robot grow more complex!

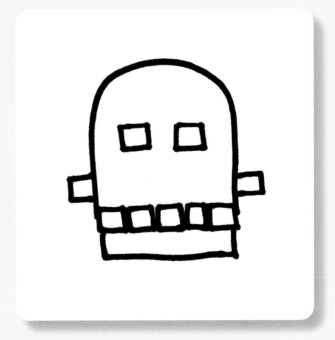

# More Fun

Bring your robot drawings to life by making 3D robots from whatever is in your recycle bin.

"Sometimes I feel almost human."

# BLIND CONTOUR PORTRAITS

It's really hard to get through this game without dissolving into giggle fits. Play this game with one other friend.

50

**1** Each player begins with a piece of paper and marker or pencil and sits across from the other.

**2** Draw the other player's portrait without lifting the pen off of the paper AND without looking at the paper.

# Tip

Don't try to make it perfect—draw fluidly and fairly quickly and follow the lines of the face with your eyes as you are drawing them on the paper.

# WEIRDO ANIMALS

It would be fun to see some of these animal hybrids running around in real life. You and a friend can do this game together, or make your own while you sit side-by-side, sneaking peeks at each other's.

**1** Roll a die to determine what the front half of the animal you draw will be:
1. Elephant
2. Monkey
3. Bird
4. Fish
5. Giraffe
6. Turtle

**2** Draw the front half.

**3** Roll again to determine the back half:
1. Snake
2. Cat
3. Ant
4. Ladybug
5. Pig
6. Lizard

**4** Draw the back half.

## More Fun

When you tire of these combinations, you can switch the "front" and "back" columns.

# EXPLORE YOUR SCRIBBLES

Scribbling is super fun in and of itself, but wait until you stare at a scribble for a while—it's like trying to find shapes in clouds!

**1** Scribble all over your page with your pencil.

**2** Hand it to your friend, who will hand you their scribble page.

**3** Look for different shapes in the scribbles and outline them in marker. Feel free to erase some of the scribbles that fall inside the marker lines if desired.

## More Fun

Vary the types of scribbles you do—try big, loopy scribbles one time and jagged, pointy scribbles the next.

# SHADOW DRAWING

This is one of my all-time favorite drawing games. First, hunt around your house for toys, mugs, utensils, and any other interestingly shaped objects you can find.

**1** Have a friend shine a flashlight on a blank wall while you hold up an object between the light and the wall. Then tape a piece of paper to the wall, centered over the shadow of the object. Trace that object on to the paper.

2 Rotate the paper on the wall and trace another object, finding interesting ways to overlap the images.

## Tip

Use different colored markers to make your drawing look really cool. Also try tracing the profile of another friend along with some objects they like to create a unique portrait of them!

3 Continue until you've traced 3 to 5 objects, depending on what looks good to you.

Chapter

3

# MIXED-MEDIA GAMES

Now that you're a little warmed up with the basic drawing games and games with friends, let's get all wild and add more art materials! It's a mixed-media drawing party right in the pages of this book.

I really tried hard not to add in anything too weird (tar, polyurethane, or dog fur), for those of you who aren't ready to become conceptual artists. In fact, I hope you might already have watercolors and colored permanent markers lying around.

Of course, a trip to the art store is always encouraged since there is no end to the fun things you will find there. Anyway...

If a game calls for a specific material you don't have on hand, or if you completely hate that material with a passion, feel free to substitute with something else.

Just like in the Simple Drawing Games chapter, branch out and see what else you can come up with after you've tried these drawing games at least once. Slow down, take your time, and explore. Enjoy the process!

# YOUR EXPLODING INTIALS

Turn your initials into an abstract design using paper, markers, and glue.

**1** Using a ruler, pencil, and scissors, measure, draw, and cut a 6 x 6 inch (15 x 15 cm) square from the page. Draw your initials in large block letters to fill the space. Color the entire design with solid colors or line designs.

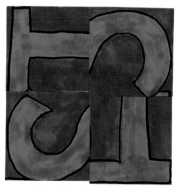

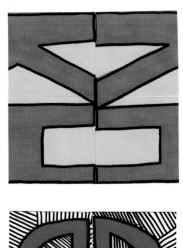

**2** Cut the square into four equal squares. Rearrange them until you have a design you like and glue them onto a piece of paper.

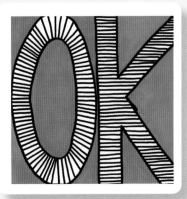

# More Fun

Cut a 9 x 9 inch (23 x 23 cm) square from a piece of paper, draw your initials, and cut it into nine equal squares. Play around with these smaller pieces to create a new design.

# MAGIC COLOR DRAWING TRANSFER

You can use crayons or oil pastels for this transfer project. Oh, and grab a ballpoint pen or pencil for the drawing part.

**A**

**B**

**1** Fold your page in half and then unfold it and lay it down flat.

**2** Draw lines of color all down the right-hand side of the page with oil pastels or crayons. The lines can go in any direction (A). Press hard so a lot of color is deposited on the page. (I usually end up snapping all the poor crayons in half with my superhuman strength.)

**3** Fold the colored half of the paper over to cover the blank half. Draw with a pen or pencil over the back of the colored page (B). Wherever you draw will transfer color onto the blank page!

### Tip

If you don't want to draw right on the back of the colored page, you can draw on another piece of paper held down on top of the page.

# GRAVITY DRAWING

You'll need a bottle of black India ink with a dropper for this game.

**1** Insert a dropper into the bottle of ink, squeeze until it's full, and drip the ink in one place on your paper.

**2** Tilt the page to move the ink around in any direction you like. Drip the ink in all different directions until your drawing is finished.

"Donut! Pizza! Candy! I must be getting hungry."

# More Fun

Try this with a friend. For an extra challenge, have your friend shout out something for you to draw right as you are dripping ink onto your page.

# CONTINUOUS LINE ANIMAL

Drawing without removing your utensil from the surface can create an unusual and interesting result. Give it a try!

66

A

B

**1** Look up the face of a favorite animal on the Internet or in a book.

**2** Draw the face on your page using one continuous line—don't lift your marker/pencil up off the page (A).

**3** When you finish drawing the animal, fill in the animal face with doodles, still without lifting your marker.

**4** Color in the face (B).

### Tip

It's more fun if you keep a smooth, even rhythm going as you are drawing your animal face. Don't start and stop; just let the marker glide around the page.

MIXED-MEDIA GAMES

# FINGERPRINT DISCOVERIES

Make random groupings of fingerprints on the page and then figure out what they remind you of.

c

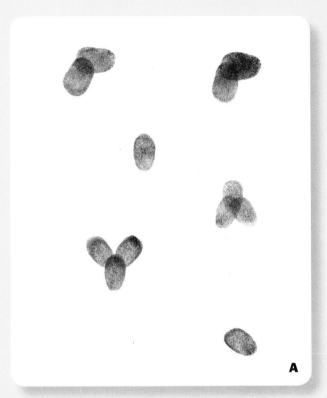

A

B

**1** Take turns with friends creating fingerprints on the page using different fingers on an inkpad and pressing them onto the page into separate groupings. Play with using the side of your finger, the very tip, etc (A).

**2** Gaze at the different groupings and see what you can draw from them (B and C).

## Tip

If you don't have an ink pad at home, you can color on your finger tip with a marker. Add more color each time you want to make a new fingerprint.

# CATALOG MODEL DRAWINGS

Catalogs would be much more fun to flip through if the models inside were like this!

**1** Cut out outfits from a clothing catalog and glue them onto different pages.

**2** Draw around the outfit to make a brand new model. I wanted to make a very fashionable dog, but I'm not sure what the other two creatures are.

"Some people think I look like a real dawg in that dress."

## Make It Silly

These models have something to say! Add speech bubbles with what they want to say to the world.

# EXQUISITE CORPSE BOOK

Exquisite Corpse is a game invented by the Surrealists in the 1920s. This game (plus the Totem Creatures [page 38] and Finish a Figure with a Friend [page 46] games) is based on this concept.

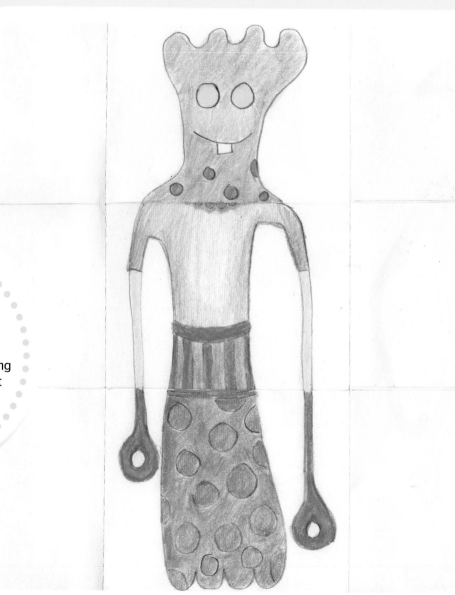

## More Fun

You can add even more figures by cutting and taping on more flaps to the front of the existing flaps.

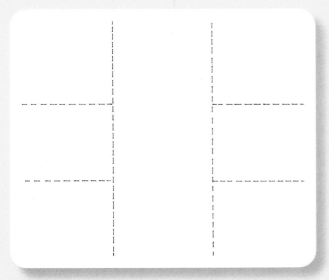

**1** Fold your page into thirds and cut the two outer flaps into three smaller flaps each. See the image above—the two big dotted lines are the fold lines, and the four small dotted lines are the cut lines.

**2** Draw a figure on the middle, uncut third of paper. You will draw the head and shoulders in the top area, the torso and arms in the middle area, and the hands and legs in the bottom area.

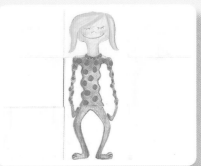

**3** One at a time, draw another figure over each of the flaps when it is closed. Make sure you line up where the head part meets the middle part and where the middle part meets the legs. You want to be able to open one flap and mix and match the parts of the characters you have drawn in order to make new characters!

# KALEIDOSCOPE CIRCLES

This game produces a work of art that looks a bit like the view through a colorful kaleidoscope. Of course, your drawing will be much cooler than a dumb old kaleidoscope.

**1** Using a can or other round object and a pencil, trace several circles all over the page. Feel free to use a couple objects of different sizes.

**2** Color in all the areas where the circles overlap.

"I'm feeling positively, positive about the negative spaces I've created."

# More Fun

Draw tangle designs in the leftover white areas.

# WHAT'S IN AN INK BLOB?

Maybe you've done ink blob drawings before, but with this one, we're going to take it a step further.

1 Fold a paper in half and drop ink drips on one side of the paper.

2 Fold the paper closed and press lightly, then open it and let it dry.

3 After the ink is totally dry, see what you can see in the ink blob shape and add to it with a marker or pen. I used a Sharpie and a white Sakura Gelly Roll pen.

"Sometimes blobs are masterpieces in the making."

# FRUIT PRINT WHEELS

Believe it or not, fruit prints make the perfect drawing starter.

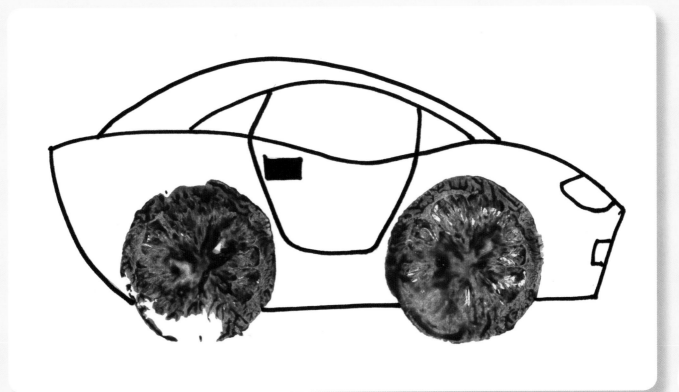

**1** Use a brayer to roll some acrylic paint or printing ink onto a palette or other flat surface (a foil-covered pan works great).

**2** Cut a lime, lemon, or orange in half and blot each half on a paper towel to remove excess moisture.

**3** Press one half of the fruit into the paint all the way and then press it onto your page to make a print. Make two prints next to each other.

**4** Turn your fruit prints into wheels by drawing some sort of vehicle around them.

## Tip

Practice making prints on scrap paper a few times until you get the hang of how much paint you need on the fruit and how hard to press the fruit onto your paper.

# FINGERPRINT SELF-PORTRAIT

Prepare to get your cute little fingers all messy while you use them in place of a marker.

**1** Sit in front of a mirror.

**2** Press your finger onto a stamp pad and dot it onto the page to "draw" yourself. Overlap more dots for darker areas.

# Tip

Start with the top of your head/hair and remember to place your eyes about halfway down your head.

"Mom and Dad will be happy. I usually use this finger to poke my little brother."

Game

# 34

# CRAYON RESIST LANDSCAPE DOODLES

Make a decorative landscape with this classic crayon resist technique.

82

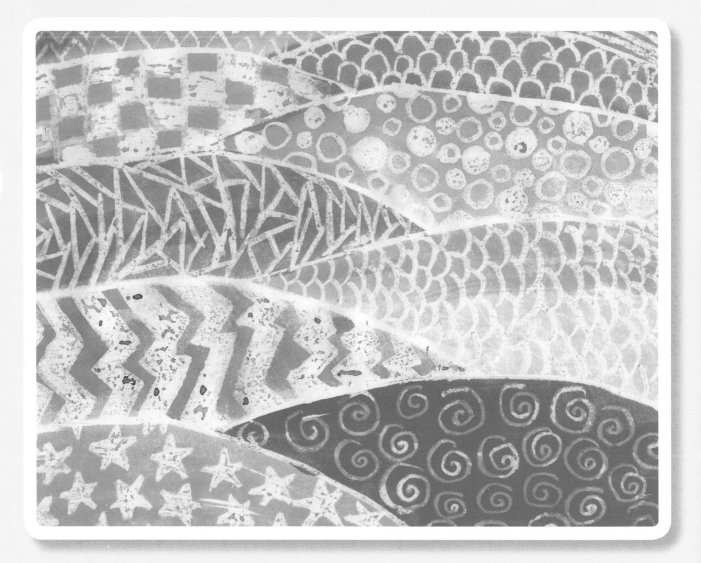

**1** Using a white crayon, cover your page in rounded hills working from the bottom of the paper to the top.

**2** Fill in each of the hills with doodles and designs.

**3** Using watercolor paint in different shades of green, brush over each of the hills.

## More Fun

Try mixing up different shades of green with your green, blue, and yellow watercolors or just make a magical rainbow landscape.

"There are more bumps in that landscape than I had on my head when I learned how to ride a skateboard."

Chapter

4

# AWESOME TANGLE GAMES

If you have not tried tangling, you are in for the treat of a lifetime. While they may look extremely hard to do, in reality, these designs are simple as pie.

They take little time to do, and they look totally rad when you're finished with them! Tangling is massively soothing and meditative. You'll find yourself in this happy state where all anxiety slips right away while you are drawing, and who doesn't like that?

I have come up with my own tangling ideas and methods. I don't think you need to limit yourself to any specific patterns, techniques, or materials. In fact, Sharpies are my pen of choice, but any waterproof markers will work just fine. While I adore professional art materials, I love the accessibility of using what's on hand. That said, do try to avoid a super-cheap pen or marker that will run out halfway through your tangling.

As you work on different tangles, you will see how the shapes of the empty spaces will help you choose your style of doodling. Fly, little birdie!

# TAPE RESIST WATERCOLOR TANGLE

With this tangle, you will use tape and watercolor paints to create negative space into which you will draw. The results look like you have designed your own craft tape!

**1** Using wide blue painter's tape, rip pieces off the roll and place them on your page in an abstract design.

**2** Watercolor over the page. In my example, I used a bright blue and a turquoise. I painted the colors on randomly, let them dry, and then painted a second layer in certain areas. Have fun playing with watercolor!

**3** After your paint has dried, carefully peel up the tape and tangle your heart out in the white areas.

# More Fun

Cut out your tangled tape areas, slap some glue on the back, and use them in a collage project, in a journal, or on your homework. Oops!

# CIRCLE TANGLES

Tangles are repetitive designs based on simple shapes, lines, and dots. Draw ones like mine to get started or just design your own. Tangle drawings are often created on a square paper tile, but as you are learning, here we do things our own way.

**88**

**1** Trace around a small bowl or roll of tape (or both) to make overlapping circles across the whole page. Make a few or a lot of circles, depending on how much tangling you want to do.

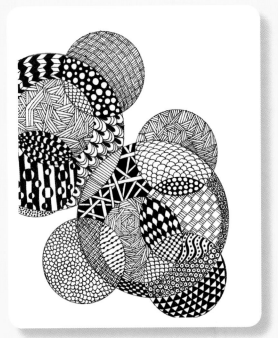

**2** Tangle the insides of the circles.

## More Fun

Try this idea again, but you can only tangle inside the circles using different styles of circles and dots.

"Despite your nerdiness, dorkhead, you sure draw a mean tangle."

"Uh, thanks (... I think)."

# DOUBLE CURSIVE TANGLES

Tangling inside words is the ultimate way to personalize your tangle. This would make a great gift for a friend!

90

**1** Hold two thin markers together and write a word or your name in cursive or block letters. Using two different colors looks cool.

**2** Tangle inside the shapes formed by the letters. You will be tangling fairly small designs and not a lot of them. Think of this as minimalistic, graphic design tangle art.

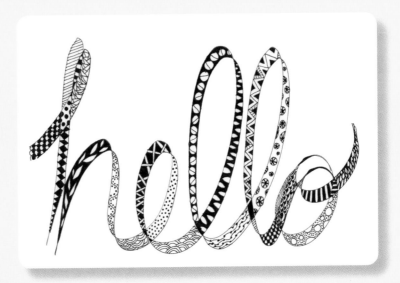

## More Fun

Try this same technique with block letters and see how you can make the tangling inside look different.

"I get lost in a sea of doodles. I can doodley-doo for hours."

# CHEVRON DESIGN TANGLE

The chevron is a very popular design element and lends itself to a more even pattern of tangling as opposed to loose tangling.

**1** Using a ruler and pencil, draw a grid of squares onto your page. (Draw lightly— you'll be erasing these later!)

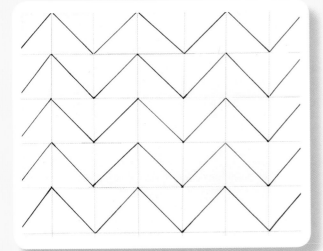

**2** Still using a ruler, draw the chevron pattern as shown. Each line starts at one corner of a box and ends at the corner diagonally across.

**3** Erase your grid lines and tangle, tangle, tangle inside the chevrons.

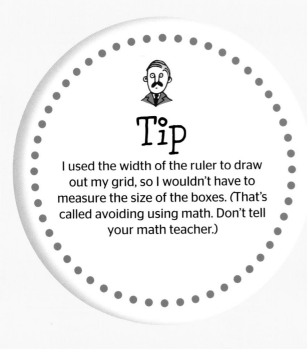

## Tip

I used the width of the ruler to draw out my grid, so I wouldn't have to measure the size of the boxes. (That's called avoiding using math. Don't tell your math teacher.)

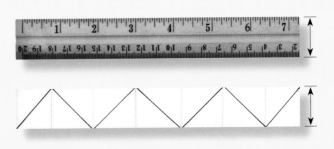

AWESOME TANGLE GAMES

# REVERSE TANGLING

I love this project! There are so many cool ways to build on this idea, so try this way and see where your imagination takes you.

**1** Cut a piece of black paper (I like black card stock) into a shape and trace it on one half of your page.

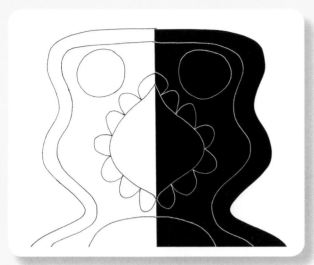

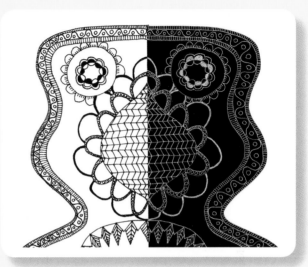

**2** Flip it over horizontally and glue it down onto your page. You will have mirror images of the black and white shapes.

**3** Tangle in the black area with a white gel pen and in the white area with a black pen. I used a Sakura Gelly Roll white ink gel pen and an Ultra Fine Sharpie.

## Make It Silly

This is starting to look like a face to me, so you could definitely turn your creation into a funny face. I wonder what tangled glasses would look like?

# ABSTRACT ART OVALS TANGLE

Watercolor meets tangling in this pretty project you can frame and hang on your wall.

1 Pick three or four colors of watercolor paint that you love together and brush some overlapping ovals onto your page.

3 Tangle inside your drawn ovals.

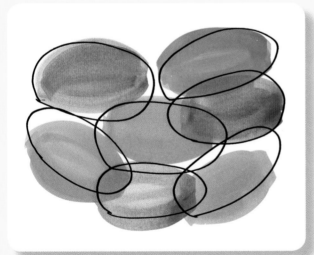

2 When they are dry, you can draw ovals over them, but don't make them perfect—they look great if they are offset from the paint ovals a bit.

# More Fun

You can make this more colorful if you use colored pens to tangle over the watercolor, but you may want to test which pen colors look good over which paint colors on a scrap of paper as you work.

Game

**41**

# RAINBOW TANGLE

I think every art project book needs a rainbow project, so here's a fun way to tangle the rainbow.

**1** Separate your page into six sections. Feel free to separate them any way you want; I happened to draw uneven stripes.

**2** Tangle in each section with the rainbow colors in order: red, orange, yellow, green, blue, and violet.

## More Fun

Make your rainbow tangle in the shape of a rainbow!

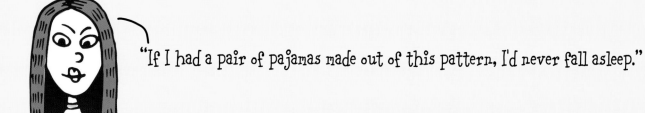

"If I had a pair of pajamas made out of this pattern, I'd never fall asleep."

# RANDOM TANGLE PAGE

I tend to be a little rigid when it comes to drawing since I really like things simple and geometric. To loosen up a little bit, I like to make tangle drawings tumbling across an entire space, with no constraints.

**1** Start your tangle loosely, without making areas to tangle within.

**2** Tangle out from there. Don't worry about where one design starts and another one ends; you can do whatever you want! Whee!

## More Fun

Try either starting at a corner of your page or in the center and tangling out from there. Or draw a random design across your page and tangle around it.

"One curl leads to another and my drawing keeps growing and growing and growing and growing and growing and gr... okay, I'll stop now."

# TANGLE QUILT

This tangle project brings a cozy, homey look to tangling. I don't recommend trying to sleep under this tangle when you're finished with it, though.

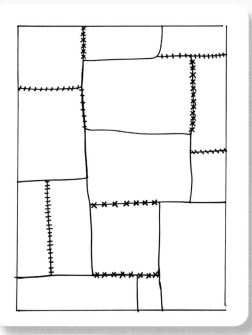

**1** Separate your page into different sizes of rectangles and squares, adding in little drawn stitch marks here and there.

**2** Tangle in each rectangle. I made mine extra colorful and filled in most of the white areas to make it look more like fabric.

"When I put my marker on the page, the designs start making themselves. Draw. Repeat. Repeat."

# Make It Silly

Some quilts are made with images sewn onto them to tell a story. Consider adding secret faces or recognizable objects here and there as part of your design.

# ICE POP STICK TANGLE

When you're short on time or just want a quick tangle fix, this is the perfect tangle project.

104

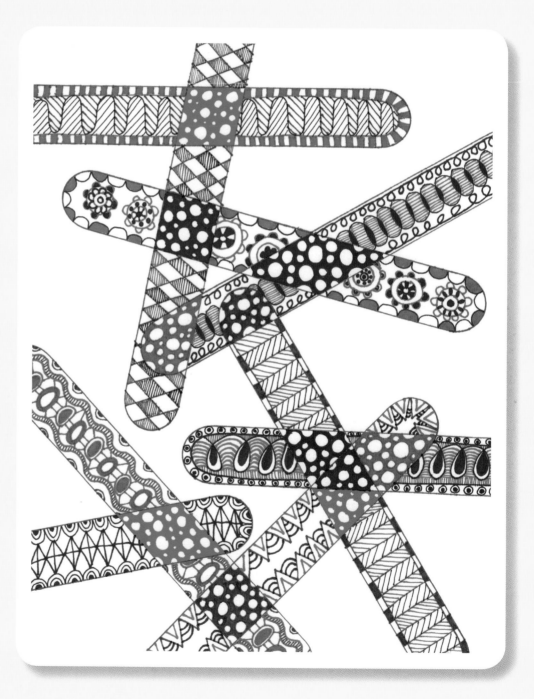

**1** Trace a jumbo ice pop stick many times, all over your page.

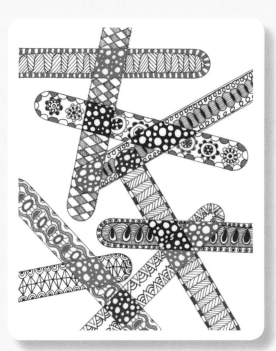

**2** Tangle in it.

**3** Eat an ice pop.

## More Fun

Do this again without overlapping the ice pop sticks. Once you've tangled your designs, cut them out to use as bookmarks. Or use Mod Podge to glue them onto jumbo ice pop sticks and secure magnets to the backs of them.

AWESOME TANGLE GAMES

# HAIR TANGLE

This is tangling taken to an all-new level of silliness.

**1** Cut out a face from a magazine or photograph and glue it onto the page.

**2** Make some wild "hair" shapes and tangle inside of them.

## More Fun

Make some of these using the faces of some of your family members and give them as gifts for birthdays or other holidays.

"If I paste this onto a piece of cardboard, this could be my Halloween costume."

Game

46

# COLLAGE ART TANGLE

Paper collage is such a fun, easy way to make a quick abstract art project. In this game, tangling adds yet another fabulous layer.

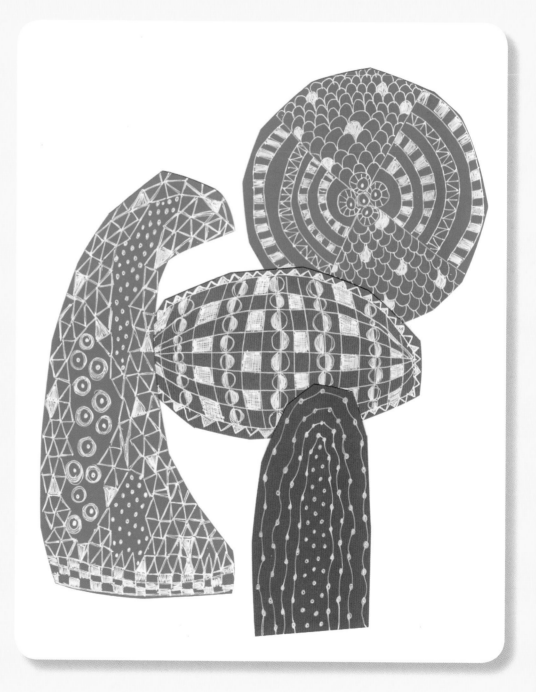

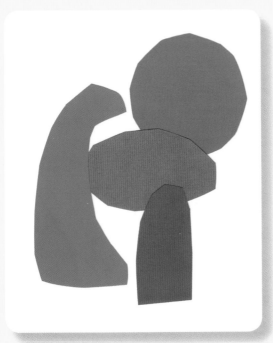

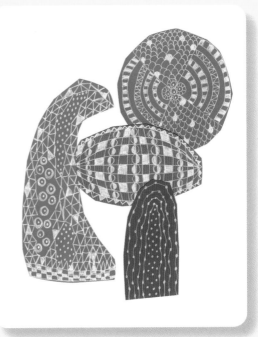

**1** Using three or four colors of card stock, cut some random shapes and glue them onto your page.

**2** Tangle on them or tangle around them—anything goes.

## More Fun

Cut out your creation and glue it to the front of a blank card. Send it to yourself in the mail with a nice note.

"Dear Me,
I love you.
Signed, Me, Myself, and I."

# About the Author

**Jeanette Nyberg** writes about art projects, cool finds, and tales of her life on her blog Craftwhack. She graduated from the Rhode Island School of Design, after which she dove into the roles of professional artist and photo stylist. Jeanette has always been fascinated by kids' natural creativity and strives to inspire a love of making in kids and adults.

# Acknowledgments

So many thanks to **Mary Ann Hall** for appearing in my life out of the blue. Your vision for this project got my creativity going a thousand fold. Thank you to the **Rockin' Art Moms**, my online tribe, creative conspirators, and BFFs. Lastly, thank you to **my family**, who showed the utmost patience and support as I went through every emotion known to man while working on this book. Love to you all.

# Also Available

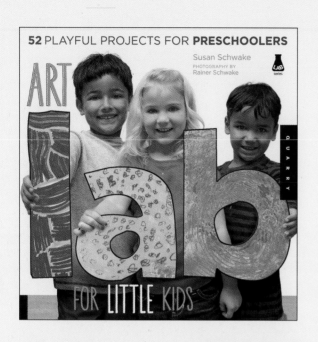

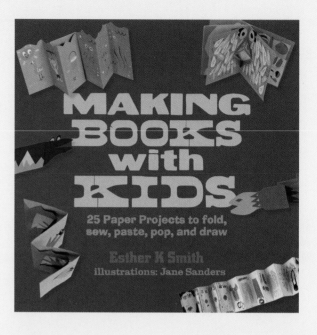